A Journey Through Poetry

A Journey Through Poetry

By

Zia Bharucha

www.whitefalconpublishing.com

A Journey Through Poetry
Zia Bharucha

www.whitefalconpublishing.com

First Edition, 2018

ISBN - 978-93-87193-88-8

About the Poet

Zia Bharucha is a teacher by profession. She has lived and worked in many parts of the world including Bombay, New York, Madeira, and Nairobi. She has also run her own business, and has been into teaching, training and preparing students in Speech and Drama and Performance Arts Examinations for Trinity College London.

She is currently writing a book reflecting on her spiritual thoughts through her life's journey.

My website is ziabharucha.com
I may be contacted at ziabharucha@gmail.com

Shachi Kale- Cover Art: Wing #1 (www.shachikale.com)

Contents

Being

Is the external you a reflection of the internal you?
Is the internal you an expression of the external you?
Does it matter?

What I feel is what I experience,
What I say is what I hear,
What I see is what I am,

Or is it all a fallacy?

I am the peace and the chaos,
I am the expanse and the contraction,
I am all and nothing,
I am waiting,
For you.

I am.

I am the observer and the experience,
I am the listener and the speaker,
I am.

I am,
Waiting,
for you.

Oneness

Oneness grows, when contradiction goes,
Togetherness begins, separation ends,
Solitude allows me TO BE.
Love flows where attention goes.

My thoughts, my words, my actions are energy and like attracts like.
What if, maybe, possibly, destroy me.
Love flows where attention goes.

My emotions consume me, distortion rules me,
Perspective heals, this moment reveals,
Love flows where attention goes.

I live, aware there is suffering,
I live, knowing I was created to be free.
My heart lives on,
Love flows where energy goes.

I am part of the whole, there is no loneliness,
Oneness is wholeness.
Love flows where attention goes.

Inspiration

I sit, I wait, I stare into the abyss,
My fingers poised, waiting

Done?

There it is, staring back at me.

Where did it come from?
Did I do this? Am I capable of this?
It flows through me and from me, but I am not it.
I am but the vessel.

Trust in it, and it will come
Force it and it will leave
Patience is key.
Enjoy the waiting, spend time engaging with life,
All will be revealed, through the pages of you.

It is fleeting like a butterfly,
It comes and goes, always leaving you wanting more.
The gift is for all, know it, ask for it.
It is yours and mine, to seek and find.

Integrity

Integrity,
Is doing the right thing regardless of its cost
to you, your well being, or your life.
It is the universal truth that needs acknowledgement,
It is not for the faint of heart nor the self indulgent.

You have choices to make, right or wrong, you make
them all day long,
If you do not stand up for what is right,
you are part of the herd being led,
Mistakes happen, deception is deliberate,
action provides the evidence.
What you do has profound consequence.

Doing what's right requires you to rise up above
yourself.
Your ego will fight it, excuses will
cloud your judgement,
Discomfort will invade you only to block you,
Shun it all and continue on.

Doing what's wrong is easy, no work required!
I, me, and myself feels wonderful, nothing else matters.
Farsightedness is extinguished for the moment.

Life is cyclical,
Hindsight is useless, guilt pointless.

Regret cannot change what is.

Suffering is created, forgiveness is required,

All, due to the lack of consciousness in a single moment.

Integrity has immense power,

It can heal, it can restore faith,

It can vindicate.

Transition

We are in constant transition.
Childhood into adulthood
Dependence to independence

Nature is in constant transition.
Abscission to flowering,
Death to rebirth.

Life is constantly changing,
Forcing adjustment,
Evolve or perish,
Are the only choices available.

There is no easy path,
No escape,
Just the eventual reality,
Everything is in transition.

We await the next phase of life.
There is a battle approaching,
Choice is key,
Time to take the leap,
No one will be exempt.

Choice

You can choose, of course you can,
We just restrict that which is available,
That's the game plan.

In a world of billions of people,
We have media controlled by a handful,
You can choose,
It's just guileful.

In a world of immense diversity,
Large companies have a monopoly,
You can choose,
It's just dishonesty.

In a world of unlimited imagination,
We have destructionism,
You have a choice,
It's isolationism.

You have choice,
We have control,
Everyone's happy
Except your soul.

Ageing

The outward journey begins only to return home,
I have to admit I love it!
I was always old on the inside,
youth held no fascination.
The young crave attention and excitement!
Love is a battle of wills, and fear a daily occurrence.

The twenties bring confusion and panic!
What do I do? Where do I go?
Every decision fraught with anxiety.

The thirties arrive with such hope!
It is the decade of upheaval,
The endless doing, coping.
The tiredness, the fighting, the pain,
the loss, the struggles,
Then,
Then there's the learning, the healing, the forgiving.
Acceptance helps with the realigning of self,
The wholeness we crave and the battle to save ME,
Is just the beginning.
Questions precede you once more,
What do I need?
What do I want?
What is my purpose?
You begin to answer them with the benefit of hindsight.

You finally begin to come into your own.

Praise be to god!

I'm finally coming home!

To me.

Waiting

Do you think being asked to wait, is a
waste of your time?
Does being made to wait, make you
feel marginalised and alone?
Do you feel embarrassed, frustrated,
stuck in no man's land.
Waiting, is time where the groundwork
of you is being laid.
Life is preparing you for what's to come.

You are incubated until you are seen as ready.
I know we all look to success as significant,
Moving ahead as vital
Transitions as pointless
You have been deceived.

Metamorphosis is necessary.
It is rooted in turning you from a
caterpillar into a butterfly.
Evolution is your winter preparing you for
your spring.
The faster you learn, understand, heal and
gain strength,
The quicker you make all else probable,
possible and achievable.

It's time to get ready,
Everything you are and ever will be is waiting for you.
Will you weather through the storm to
get there, or will you give up?

If you can see past the waiting,

It's yours.

Nirvana

I travel around the world, looking for something,
What will fill this emptiness within me?
I look for it in material things, clothes,
shoes, bags, cars, yachts, jewellery.
Nothing.

Will I find it in money? Perhaps,
Relationships? Perhaps,
Temporarily.
I feel empty.
What will fill me, fulfil me?

I yearn for something, what is IT?
Will I know it when I see it? Can I catch it,
grasp it, hold it? Will it leave me, if I don't
recognise it?

I need you, even though I don't know you.
I wait hoping you will show up to rescue me.
Where are you? What are you?

Silence reveals you, I hear you whisper, you are within?
Why didn't you say so?
All this time I spent searching for you and you
were where I never dared look, you were
where I never dare venture,
WITHIN.

Here we are together, reunited,
I understand now, I am, that which I crave,
I am Nirvana.

Life

Who are you?
Are you your name and profession? Your features?

What defines you?
Are you your likes and dislikes? Your fears and fancies?

What are you?
Are you your talents? Your hopes and dreams?

Who are you?
If I strip it all away.

I,
I am the internal you, not the external you.
I am love. I am consciousness.

You?
You are not your body, you are not your thoughts,
you are not your experiences, you are
not your achievements.

You are love. You are consciousness.

I am one with everything in the universe.
The sun, the stars, the planets, the oceans,
the birds, the sky, the earth.
I am part of the whole and the whole is a part of me.
I am a part of you, you are a part of me.

We are on this journey of life together,
I am the teacher, you are the student.

I am experiencing myself through you, through your
creativity, through your perspective,
through your choices.

You experience me as love, as peace, as joy, as silence.
I am here because of you, you are here because of me.

In this reality I help you AWAKEN.
In this reality you help me experience life,
In this reality I help you heal your wounds,
In this reality you help set me free.

Life is a journey of discovery, of healing, of knowing.
I am your guide and you are the traveller
Let's begin,
Life is waiting.

Hope

Is hope an illusion?
Or a delusion?
A collusion,
That leads to confusion.
Is it a marketing tool,
To fool and rule.

Hope, is despair,
Repackaged, with fear,
To steer the sincere.

It is deferring,
What's occurring,
Yet yearning.

This moment is both hopeful and fearful,
We are in the middle.
It is suspenseful,
Yet, be careful.

Be not swayed,
Nor dismayed,
You have an aide.
He is with you,
Be unafraid.

There will be malaise,
There will be delays.
Continue with praise,
And you will be amazed.

Appreciate everyday and
Pray you will never, never be led astray.

Love

Is it love that causes me to shed a tear for your pain?
Is it love that makes me, humane?
My heart aches for the agony you sustain.

Is it love that helps me understand the fragility of me?
I break apart,
Pray for a fresh start.
A sweetheart,
To restart,
My heart.

Love is what holds,
Whilst chaos unfolds,
Behold.
There may be strife,
Let love, be the elixir of life.

Feelings

I wilt under constant negativity,
It breaks me, turns me inside out,
I am no longer myself, just a hollowed out carcass.

I descend into meanness, rudeness, sarcasm,
I struggle to breathe,
It seeps into me, into my every thought,
every emotion, every action,
I long to be different.

I blossom under positivity,
It transforms me, turns me inside out,
I am myself, revealed to be already whole,
I am lifted into engaging, caring and loving.

I exhale,
It seeps into me, into my every thought,
every emotion, every action.

I am free to BE
If you are being pulled apart, you are not alone.
Live negatively and lose, live positively and win.
Duality divides, the oneness of you.

Happy, Unhappy

I am happy!
IF I get what I want, and do what I want.

I am unhappy!
IF I get what I want, and do what I want.

I oscillate between the two, all day long.
Is this all there is?

Asking the question, opens pandora's box.
There is a way out,
Awareness, is the answer.

There is no happiness nor unhappiness,
Perception allows us to see, there is no duality.
There is only oneness.

Life does not need to be perfect,
It doesn't require getting what you
want, or doing what you want.

Oneness is the key, to ending the oscillation,
Of the happy unhappy me.

Anger

Anger separates you from yourself,
It divides you.

It is not me, that yells.
It is not me that seethes in silence.
It is not me that loses it.

I am the awareness.
I am the calm under the storm,
I am the voice of peace.

The angry seem to be inflicting upon the earth, their
way of doing, being and seeing.
Those who respond in support will bear responsibility.
Peace within, peace flowing out.

We have a choice and the world will reflect this.
Calm or storm?
Anger or peace?
You or the annihilation of you?

Fear

It impersonates me,
It tries to rule me,
I allow it.

It breeds chaos within me,
It kills rational thought,
I allow it.

Sweaty palms,
Pounding chest,
Irrational thought,

I allow it.

Fear, is a feeling.
It requires awareness and confrontation.
Acceptance bursts its bubble.

It is a tool used to manipulate me,
It is an illusion used to control me,
Do I allow it?

I am afraid, I admit it.
I have no control, I admit it.

No longer will I be at its mercy,
No longer will I worry over it's wrath,
My emotions can be contained,
My fear acknowledged.

I am me, laid bare.
Strengthened through my weakness,
Ready, to face another day.

Faith

I trust in that which I can see, hear and feel,
I trust in you.

You disappoint me.
In my despair I do not see,
I disappoint you, too.

Where do we go from here?
In whom do we trust?

Humans are fallible,
God, is perfection.

He will not abandon you,
He will not judge you.

He is the space that heals,
He is the quiet that reveals,
He is the peace that understands
He is the faith that guides.

You are never alone,
You are always listened to,
You are forgiven for
You are loved.

I trust in that which is unseen, unheard and unfelt.
I trust in him, my lord.

Evil

Evil is not the bad within you.
It is the intentional decision to stick with a
bad ideologue, long after its expiration,
Regardless of consequences.

Evil is not the bad within you.
It is allowing the negative you, to run free,
without constraints, repudiating good,
Regardless of consequences.

Evil is not the bad within you.
It is the lack of understanding, acceptance,
humility and forgiveness.
It is trying to be god, when you're only human,
Regardless of consequences.

When will we understand that good and bad is within,
in equal measure,
It is a choice given to you, which will you choose?

Life is the pathway to learning,
It is a tough road, not for the faint.

Every turn offers choice,
Every choice requires a decision,
Every decision requires thought,
Every thought requires knowledge.

Knowledge that you know nothing,
You control nothing,
You are on a journey of discovery,
The discovery of you,
Of the good, that is you.

Sharing

I can only share what's mine,
I open my heart and you receive.
Giving with expectation, is receiving with burden.

Is it really mine? Nothing has a sign on it?
Ownership changes hands,
What's mine today is yours tomorrow.

If I hold on tight to what is mine,
And you do the same,
What we miss is the purpose of creation.

I came with nothing and I will leave the same.
Selfishness is like toasting death during life.

Creation has provided more than enough for all,
Greed does not.
Life has lost its meaning, we have gone astray.

Share without fear
Care without limits
The largesse within you,
Still believes.

Control

BOY!
Do as I ask,
Live as I say,
Obey me!

Yes father.

Son, what is the matter with you?
You do nothing, you say nothing,
your life is going nowhere.
MAN UP!

Yes father.

Grown up, now.

Distance requires a change of tactics.
Orders morph into unsolicited advice,
Threats into guilt.

I obey you but you blame me,
I disappoint you but you made me,
I don't understand what you want from me?

I am you.

Judgement

You judge me.
My looks
My wealth
My home

Life feels burdensome, relentless.

I judge you.
Your job
Your relationships
Your life

I feel empowered.

I am not able to comprehend your life and it's difficulties,
You are unwilling to hear me.
Where there is judgement,
There cannot be understanding.

Unless the layers of illusion are wiped away,
The real you and the real me stay away.
Trust is key,
To preserving the true, you and me.

I do not want your advice,
I do not want your condescension,
I do not want your negativity,
I do not want constant discussion.

I do not have the answers,
I do not know the questions
I want peace
I want quiet
I want god.

Enjoyment

Dawn breaks, the birds are gliding,
The leaves glisten in the sunshine,
I watch in silence without thought,
Appreciation fills me.

Do you feel my gratitude?

Are you awake?
Do you acknowledge its beauty?
Every minute brings the opportunity
For enjoyment.

Life is awakening,
Life is creating,
Are you watching?
You are it, and it is you,
Inexorably linked.

Enjoyment is taking a hot bath on a cold day,
It's shopping, cooking and eating a meal,
It's gratitude for every breath,
It's each and every moment,
Don't let it pass without acknowledgement.

Dusk breaks and all things glow in its beauty

Darkness envelopes everything

It's time for contemplation

Rest beckons,

Do you feel my gratitude?

Entertainment

We are at the circus, Ladies and Gentlemen,
It's time for MAGIC! Now you
see it and now you don't!
It's Deception, Diversion, Distraction.
What did I miss?

When the world is too much,
Come to me.
When you need thoughtless time,
Come to me.
When you need a refill of happiness,
Come to me.
When you need to feel better,
I am here.

I have the power to take you away,
The stress,
The burden,
The numbing tiredness,
Have no fear, I am here.

I'm your freedom, your escape,
Your flight of fantasy,
Embrace me.

We are at the circus, ladies and gentlemen,
It's time for MAGIC! Now you
see it and now you don't!
It's deception, diversion, distraction.
What did I miss? What did I miss? What did I miss?

Celebrations

Do celebrations require occasions?
Is perspective all you need?

We live in the valley, looking up at the mountain peaks,
Hoping,
Reaching,
Striving.

The mountain creaks with the weight of our desires,
It descends
Into the valley,
Valley into the sea.

What a disaster!
All is lost.
We long for what was
The opportunities lost in the whisper of moments.

Is perspective all you need to celebrate?

Upside Down

Lies are truth, bad is good,
We live in the upside down neighborhood.

Artificial is natural, innocent are now guilty,
This is the new upside down committee.

Rude is the new polite, stupidity is now considered smart,
We are at the upside down contempt of court.

Cruel is the new humane, supporter is now opponent,
We are facing the upside down agent.

Division is now unity, violence is the new form
of surrender,
We are in the upside down battle center.

We are distanced from ourselves,
Everything's blurred,
There is no sky and earth,
We need a spiritual rebirth.

There is no god, no need for restraint,
I am lost. I need constraint.

I have been ravaged,
Help, is all I can salvage.

Privacy

I give you information about myself,
My address, my family, my friends, my places of interest,
I share my life.
I have made the private me, public.

WHY?

You know what I read, where I go, what I watch, what I do, who I call,
You know me.
You make the public me, private.

WHY?

I am in prison.
The walls are my country's borders.

Whose fault is it?

Division

Black or white,
Let's unite.
Rich or poor,
Let's confer.

You and me have a long history,
Yes we do.
There has been a lot of misery,
That is true.

Do you think people are ready to move forward?
If offered,
A chance to end the repression,
The aggression,
The misinformation?

Can we change?
Without a shooting exchange?
What is the answer,
That won't spell disaster.

When we begin to understand,
Hand in hand,
We are the same.
The blame game
Can end,
And we can begin to transcend.

Division is a decision,
Driven,
To arouse suspicion.

There is no difference,
Just ignorance.
We will come undone,
If we do not understand that we are all one.

Information War

The fight is on.
Who controls it?
Who directs it?
Who writes it?

It's ours to manoeuvre.

The fight is on.
Truth or lies,
Biased or unbiased,
Right or wrong,

It's ours to manoeuvre.

Information written and rewritten,
Truth twisted and mauled,
Facts immaterial.

It's ours to manoeuvre.

Reality hidden.
We kill,
We inflict pain,
We burn down.

No harm done. RIGHT?

Money GOD

We worship it, we kneel at its feet,
Ask for more and more of it,
For it's the key to happiness.

When given it we feel blessed and special,
We use it to wield the world into our image,
The money GOD keeps on giving,
May he never turn his back on us.

He has changed course,
I cry
I beg
I plead
The god of money has turned away,
I am lost.

I turn my back on HIM,
He was never the source of my happiness,
He never made me special,
I am already, whole.

What a revelation it has been.
I am ok, still
I know one day you will change course once more,
And it will be my turn, again.

This time I will not mistake you for me,
This time I will share you,
This time you will not define me,
For I know I am already,
WHOLE.

Drum Beats

Do you hear the drum beats?
I have pronouncements to make!
Hear ye, hear ye,
I come bearing news.
Listen to me, follow me,
Accept what I say,
I only ever do, what is best for you!

Do you hear the drum beats?
Do you not love the sound?
Do you not feel the rhythm?
Allow yourself to fall deeper and deeper into its trance,
Let go, I'm here to hold you, guide you, lead you.

Do you hear the drum beats?
I am being herded towards the sound.
Where am I? I ask knowing it's too late,
I am already at death's door.

Did you not hear the drum beats?
You were supposed to run from the sound!
Why was I so foolish not to see
What was always in plain sight,
The drumbeats were a warning,
To one and all.

www.ingramcontent.com/pod-product-compliance
Ingram Content Group UK Ltd.
Pitfield, Milton Keynes, MK11 3LW, UK
UKHW042001190726
13854UKWH00005B/2096

9 789387 193888